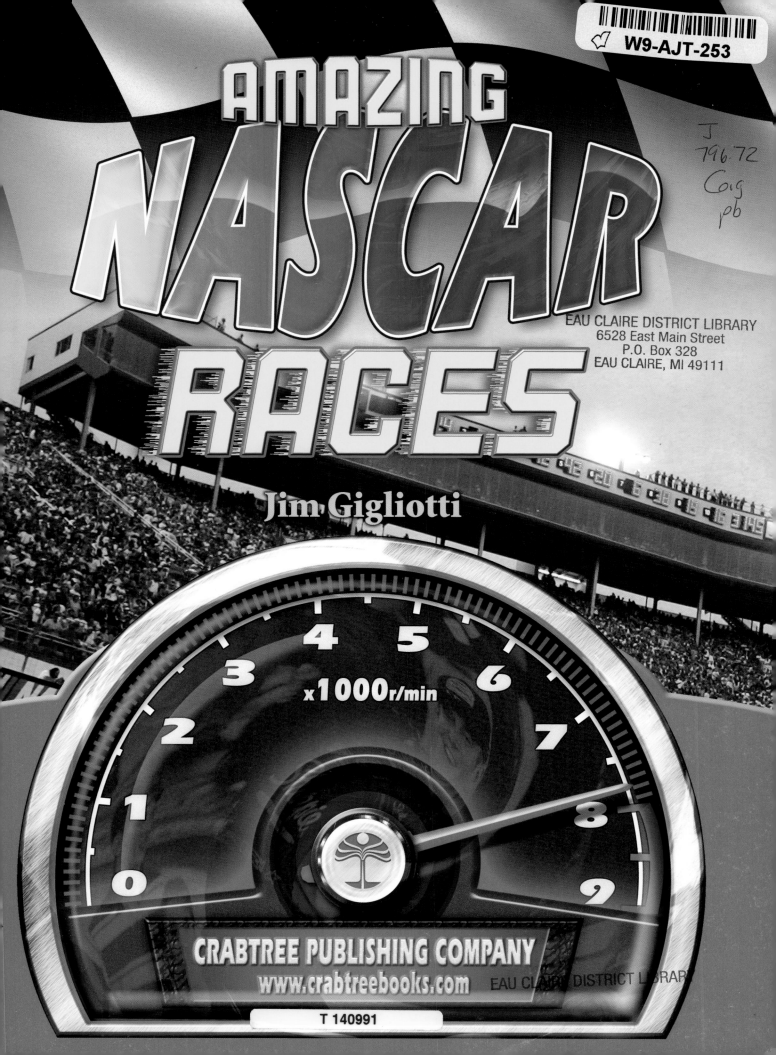

AMAZING
NASCAR
RACES

Jim Gigliotti

x1000r/min

CRABTREE PUBLISHING COMPANY
www.crabtreebooks.com

Crabtree Publishing Company

www.crabtreebooks.com

Coordinating editor
Chester Fisher

Series and project editor
Shoreline Publishing Group LLC

Author
Jim Gigliotti

Project Manager
Kavita Lad (Q2AMEDIA)

Art direction
Rahul Dhiman (Q2AMEDIA)

Design
Ranjan Singh (Q2AMEDIA)

Cover Design
Ravijot Singh (Q2AMEDIA)

Photo research
Anasuya Acharya & Amit Tigga
(Q2AMEDIA)

Manuscript development and photo research
assistance provided by Shoreline Publishing
Group LLC, Santa Barbara, California

Acknowledgments

The publishers would like to thank the following for
permission to reproduce photographs:

AP Photo: pages 10, 11; John Bazemore: page 27 (bottom);
David Boe: page 31; Russ Hamilton: page 21; Terry Renna:
page 5; Bob Self: page 16; Glenn Smith: pages 6, 9
Bettmann/Corbis: page 17
Worthy Canoy/NASCAR: page 29
Bill Hall/Getty Images: page 26
John Harrelson/Getty Images for NASCAR: page 24
Rusty Jarrett/Getty Images for NASCAR: page 15
Joe Robbins: cover, title page, pages 4, 7, 8, 13, 14, 18-20,
22, 23, 27 (middle right), 28, 30
Jamie Squire/Nascar Media: page 25
State Library and Archives of Florida: page 12

Cover: Bristol Motor Speedway, Bristol

Title page: Bristol Motor Speedway, Bristol.

Library and Archives Canada Cataloguing in Publication

Gigliotti, Jim
    Amazing NASCAR races / Jim Gigliotti.

(NASCAR)
ISBN 978-0-7787-3191-7 (bound).--ISBN 978-0-7787-3199-3 (pbk.)

    1. NASCAR (Association)--History--Juvenile literature. 2. Stock car
racing--United States--History--Juvenile literature. I. Title. II. Series: NASCAR
(St. Catharines, Ont.)

GV1029.9.S74G525 2008   j796.720973   C2007-907375-1

Library of Congress Cataloging-in-Publication Data

Gigliotti, Jim.
    Amazing NASCAR races / Jim Gigliotti.
        p. cm. -- (NASCAR)
    Includes index.
    ISBN-13: 978-0-7787-3191-7 (rlb)
    ISBN-10: 0-7787-3191-X (rlb)
    ISBN-13: 978-0-7787-3199-3 (pb)
    ISBN-10: 0-7787-3199-5 (pb)
    1. Stock car racing--United States--Juvenile literature. 2. NASCAR
(Association)--Juvenile literature. I. Title.

GV1029.9.S74G523 2008
796.72--dc22
                                                    2007049020

Crabtree Publishing Company

www.crabtreebooks.com   1-800-387-7650

Published in Canada
Crabtree Publishing
616 Welland Ave.
St. Catharines, ON
L2M 5V6

Published in the United States
Crabtree Publishing
PMB16A
350 Fifth Ave., Suite 3308
New York, NY 10118

Published in the United Kingdom
Crabtree Publishing
White Cross Mills
High Town, Lancaster
LA1 4XS

Published in Australia
Crabtree Publishing
386 Mt. Alexander Rd.
Ascot Vale (Melbourne)
VIC 3032

Contents

Amazing!

Whether a NASCAR race ends in a tight finish or amid the flying metal of wrecked cars or with the winner comfortably ahead, every race has the chance to become among the sport's most memorable.

Memories are Made

NASCAR driver Kevin Harvick had just beaten Mark Martin in a furious race to the finish line in the season-opening 2007 Daytona 500. It was one of the most incredible finishes in **stock car** racing history. "Man, this is the Daytona 500!" Harvick said in amazement after the famous race. "Can you believe it?" Lots of fans were just as excited after a dramatic race that they'll remember for a long time. Just like they were the time that Jeff Gordon held off Dale Earnhardt Sr. to win at Daytona. Or the time that Earnhardt came from way back in the pack to win at Talladega. Or the time that a young Kurt Busch sealed his first NASCAR title on the final day of the first NASCAR playoff "Chase" in 2004. Or...well, you get the idea. There are lots more races just like the ones we've already mentioned. You'll find many of their stories in this book.

Kevin Harvick's nickname is "Happy"—he sure was after winning the Daytona 500.

What Makes a Great Race

Why were these races chosen for this book? Well, some were picked for their historical importance, like the very first official NASCAR race in 1948 or the first Daytona 500 in 1959 or the Brickyard 400 in 1994 (the first time that stock cars ever raced at the famous Indianapolis Motor Speedway). Some were picked because the winning drivers overcame long odds or made big comebacks, like when Dale Earnhardt roared back from way behind to win the Winston 500

A great finish makes a great race—but there are other reasons races are memorable, too.

in 2000. Some were picked for how they determined a season champion, like when Alan Kulwicki (1992) or Kurt Busch (2004) won their titles in the last race of the season. And some were selected simply because a fantastic finish— like the one in the 2007 Daytona 500—keeps them in the memories of NASCAR fans. What's your favorite NASCAR race?

The Great American Race

If a NASCAR fan could pick only one race to watch each year, it would be the Daytona 500. Since 1959, this 500 mile (804.7 km), slam-bang spectacular has produced a garage full of memories.

NASCAR's Big Day

Most sports gradually build to a high point, with their most important event at the end of the season. That's true with baseball and the World Series or pro football and the Super Bowl. But not NASCAR. Stock car racing's most important event, the Daytona 500, comes right at the beginning of the season. Every team is fresh from the off-season and ready to go! The Daytona 500 is so big that sometimes it's called "the Super Bowl of NASCAR." More often, it's called the "Great American Race." It's the race that every NASCAR fan wants to see more than any other, and it's the race that every NASCAR driver wants to win more than any other. With so much riding on the outcome every year, it's little wonder that the event has produced many of NASCAR's best, and most famous, races. Here are a few of them.

There's nothing quite like the colors, sights, and sounds of Daytona International Speedway on race day.

Door-to-Door in 2007

Kevin Harvick won his first Daytona 500 in 2007 after an unbelievable finish that is sure to be remembered as long as they run the race. Mark Martin, a popular **veteran** driver who was still looking for his first Daytona 500 win at age 48, was out in front on the last turn of the last lap, with Harvick in close pursuit. Suddenly, a huge wreck unfolded behind the two leaders as they frantically sprinted door-to-door to the finish. The yellow **caution flag** came out just after Harvick nosed past Martin by inches at the finish line—or, in terms of time, by just two-hundredths of a second. One car involved in the wreck even followed the leaders across the line upside down on its hood! "It was the wildest thing I've been part of in a long time," Harvick said.

On-the-Job Training

Kevin Harvick was supposed to race only a handful of times as a **rookie** in the 2001 season before easing into the NASCAR Cup series full-time in 2002. But he was pushed into the spotlight after Dale Earnhardt was killed in a tragic crash during the season-opening 2001 Daytona 500. That race is memorable for all the wrong reasons. Michael Waltrip won, but the legendary Earnhardt died when he went into the wall on the last turn of the last lap.

Kevin Harvick's No. 29 car barely beats Mark Martin and the No. 01 car at Daytona in '07.

Dale Earnhardt Sr. is out in front at the Daytona 500 in 1998. He went on to win.

The 20th Time is the Charm!

After 20 years of trying, Dale Earnhardt Sr. finally won the Daytona 500 in 1998. He had many close calls before, but some misfortune always kept him from winning. One year, he looked as if he was going to win, but then he ran out of gas. Another year, he was about to win until he blew out a tire. Finally, in 1998, he took the checkered flag at Daytona. It wasn't exactly dramatic—it came under a caution flag. But it was emotional. After Earnhardt's victory, the other drivers and many of their crew members lined up to congratulate the **sentimental** favorite. After all, while they didn't always like "The **Intimidator's**" tactics, they always respected him.

Running on Empty

Three-time NASCAR champion Darrell Waltrip was another of stock car racing's most popular drivers during his career. He waited almost as long as Dale Earnhardt Sr. did to win at Daytona. Waltrip, in car No. 17, won the 500 in his 17th start in 1989. He did it despite running out of gas on the last lap—he crossed the finish line on fumes. According to a NASCAR official after the race, the gas left in Waltrip's tank "wouldn't fill a thimble."

Youth Wins Over Experience

One year after Dale Earnhardt finally won the Daytona 500, it looked as if he might be in line for another victory. But a young Jeff Gordon held off Earnhardt over the final 10 laps of the '99 race to win by one car length. Gordon was only 27, and was competing in the Daytona 500 for just the seventh time. He made a **gutsy** move in between leader Rusty Wallace and Ricky Rudd late in the race to move into first place. But then he saw "The Intimidator" in his rearview mirror! Earnhardt tried everything he could—including a little "love tap" on Gordon's rear bumper—but he couldn't get past the youngster over the final 10 laps. Gordon won a race that thrilled the drivers as well as the spectators. "It was intense and exciting from where I was sitting," Gordon said afterward.

Jeff Gordon (No. 24) held off Dale Earnhardt Sr. to the finish line at Daytona in 1999.

All in the Family

It's no surprise that NASCAR's most famous racing family—the Petty family—has been in the thick of some of the most famous Daytona 500 races.

The King and the Fox

The two drivers with the most wins in NASCAR history, Richard Petty (who was also known as "The King") and David Pearson ("The Fox"), battled down to the wire in the 1976 Daytona 500. Late in the race, the lead went back and forth— Petty was out in front, then Pearson, then Petty again. With the crowd on its feet and roaring, the two legends came to the last lap of the race still running first and second. One of them was sure to win. Suddenly, they crashed on the final turn of the final lap. Petty's car stalled just short of the finish line. He tried over and over to get it started, but he couldn't. Pearson's car was also badly damaged, but he kept it running. Petty could only watch with disappointment and surprise as Pearson crossed the finish line as fast as his wrecked car could go— about 20 miles (32 km) per hour!

Fight to the Finish

Three years later, at the 1979 Daytona 500, Richard Petty won after another last-lap crash. This time, the crash knocked out the leaders, Cale Yarborough and Donnie Allison. As Petty was taking the checkered flag, Yarborough and Bobby Allison (Donnie's brother and a fellow driver) got into a fight at the scene of the wreck. It was captured by cameras on national television!

While Richard Petty couldn't get the No. 43 car to start again, David Pearson was slowly crossing the finish line to win the 1976 Daytona 500.

That's Lee Petty in car. No. 42 and Johnny Beauchamp in No. 73 at Daytona in 1959. They finished just about this close, too!

Photo Finish

Nearly half a century after the first Daytona 500 in 1959, that race remains one of the best in NASCAR history. The race featured it all: drama, excitement, and **controversy**. Here's what happened: Lee Petty (Richard Petty's dad and a three-time NASCAR champion) and Johnny Beauchamp raced side-by-side toward the checkered flag. They crossed the finish line at just about the same time. But a third driver did, too! It was Joe Weatherly, who was in a car that was one lap behind the leaders. The officials couldn't tell who won. At first, they declared Beauchamp the winner. Beauchamp even posed for photographs with the winner's trophy. But Petty thought he had won. So NASCAR said that the results were unofficial. Three days later, after reviewing photos and TV footage, NASCAR determined that Petty actually had won the race by a mere 24 inches (61 cm).

The Most Checkered Flags at Daytona

Every NASCAR driver dreams of winning the Daytona 500. These are the only men who have lived that dream more than once:

Driver	Wins
Richard Petty	7
Cale Yarborough	4
Bobby Allison	3
Jeff Gordon	3
Dale Jarrett	3
Bill Elliott	2
Sterling Marlin	2
Michael Waltrip	2

History-Making Races

Just about every NASCAR race is memorable for one reason or another. Certainly, it's memorable to the driver who won it! But some races are a little extra special for the role that they play in NASCAR history. Let's start at the beginning.

The First Meeting

Late in 1947, Bill France and some other drivers got together in Daytona Beach, Florida, to bring some organization to stock car races. Up until then, races were run independently at tracks in the South. There were no common rules, **governing body**, or national champion. Another problem was dishonest race promoters. Sometimes, they would promise a certain amount of money to the race winner. Once the race was over, though, the promoter was gone—with the money from ticket sales! Out of that meeting, NASCAR was born. NASCAR stands for the National Association for Stock Car Auto Racing. It has been run by the France family since the beginning.

The First Race

On February 15, 1948, NASCAR held its first official race. It was on a 2.2 mile (3.5 km) beach road course in Daytona Beach, Florida. Fifty-six drivers competed in the Rayson Memorial for the $1,000 first-place money. Red Byron won. (Byron was a World War II veteran who had been injured during the fighting. He had to wear a special brace that was attached to the clutch to support his leg). Byron won with an average speed of 75.7miles (121.8 km) per hour. NASCAR was on the road to success.

Red Byron won the first official NASCAR race in 1948. He also went on to become the first season points champion one year later.

The Start of the Cup Series

The next year, in June of 1949, NASCAR began running a series of races to determine a national champion. Points were awarded to drivers based on what place they finished in a race. At the end of the season, the winner was called the Grand National champion. Today, the same kind of system crowns the winner of the Sprint Cup.

In a strange twist, the first man to cross the finish line in a Cup Series race wasn't the winner! Glenn Dunnaway originally appeared to win that race in Charlotte, North Carolina. Later, though, he was disqualified for using an illegal **chassis**. So Jim Roper was the official winner, even though he finished three laps behind Dunnaway. By the way, Roper earned $2,000 for his win. That was a large sum of money in those days. But compare it with Kevin Harvick, who earned $1,510,469 for his team when he won the Daytona 500 in 2007!

Richard Petty and his No. 43 car are number one in all-time Cup Series victories.

All-Time Wins Leaders

In 1948, Jim Roper was the first man to win an official Cup series event. Here are the drivers with the most career NASCAR Cup Series victories:

Driver	Wins
Richard Petty	200
David Pearson	105
Bobby Allison	84
Darrell Waltrip	84
Cale Yarborough	83
*Jeff Gordon	79
Dale Earnhardt, Sr.	76
Rusty Wallace	55
Lee Petty	54
Ned Jarrett	50
Junior Johnson	50

*entering 2008

Jeff Gordon (car No. 24) surges past Ernie Irvan (No. 28) en route to winning the Brickyard 400 in 1994.

The Brickyard

Indianapolis, Indiana, is the heart of Indy-car country. Indy cars are much different from stock cars. They are **open-wheel**, open-**cockpit** cars. The most famous open-wheel race in America is the Indy 500, which has been held at the Indianapolis Motor Speedway since the early 1900s. Before 1994, the historic track had never hosted a stock car race. But that year, NASCAR came to town. On August 6, 1994, the first Brickyard 400 was held at the Indianapolis Motor Speedway. Since then, the Brickyard 400 has become one of the biggest races on the stock car schedule.

A Dream Come True

Jeff Gordon won the first Brickyard 400. That was fitting, because he used to drive by the Indianapolis Motor Speedway and dream of racing there. He just never thought that it would be in a stock car! Gordon is one of the best NASCAR drivers of the current era—or any era. He grew up in northern California racing quarter-midget cars, go-karts, and sprint cars (all smaller and lighter than big NASCAR stock cars). When he was a teenager, though, his family moved to Indiana, to a place called Pittsboro. That's not too far from Indianapolis. So Gordon started driving Indy-style, open-wheel racecars. Gordon soon shifted to stock cars, but there was no NASCAR race in Indianapolis when he was a full-time rookie in the Cup Series in 1993.

NASCAR in Indy Country

In 1994, though, NASCAR held a race at the famous Indianapolis Motor Speedway for the first time. Gordon knew he wanted to be the first driver to win the Brickyard 400. But so did a lot of other drivers. "You're gonna remember who won the first Brickyard," three-time NASCAR champion Darrell Waltrip said before the race. It turned out to be a great race. About 300,000 fans were there to see it. Defending season champ Dale Earnhardt Sr. hit the wall on the very first lap. (He stayed in the race and finshed fifth). Rusty Wallace, Ernie Irvan, and Gordon kept passing the lead back and forth late in the day. Finally, five laps from the end, it was Gordon and Irvan in a side-by-side duel. Gordon decided that it was now or never if he was going to have any chance to win the race. He made his move, zooming past Irvan to take the lead. Then, suddenly, Irvan's right front tire went flat.

Gordon was home free. (Irvan fell back all the way to 17th place). When the race was over, Gordon celebrated by taking two victory laps around the Brickyard, instead of the traditional one lap. He was crying so many tears of joy that he wanted to stop crying before he got out of the car and faced the cameras! "The Daytona 500 is our biggest event," he later said. "But I don't know if any win will ever top that first Brickyard 400."

Man for All Seasons

The Indianapolis Motor Speedway hosts the Brickyard 400, the Indy 500, and the United States Grand Prix. Only one man has raced in all three events at "The Brickyard." That's Juan Pablo Montoya, an Indy Car veteran who was a NASCAR rookie in 2007.

Juan Pablo Montoya has been driving racecars for a long time, but he was a rookie on the NASCAR circuit (in car No. 42) in 2007.

July 4th Spectacular!

The Firecracker 400 was a race that used to be held on July 4—no matter what day of the week it was. Few races in NASCAR history have produced the fireworks that the famous race did in 1984.

No. 200

Richard Petty won seven NASCAR championships and more Cup series races than any other driver in history. He's a member of the National Motorsports Hall of Fame, and he was named to NASCAR's list of the 50 Greatest Drivers when the organization celebrated its 50th anniversary in 1998. He won the Daytona 500 a record seven times. But midway through the 1984 season, the man they call "The King" was stuck on 199 victories in his storied career. He desperately wanted to reach 200. Petty got that win at the Firecracker 400 at Daytona in 1984 under a yellow caution flag. Despite—or because of—the caution, this event featured one of

the most exciting finishes ever to a NASCAR race. The rules at the time allowed drivers to sprint to the finish line after a caution (it's illegal now). In the Firecracker 400, there was a crash two laps from the finish. That meant that the race would end under caution. Petty and Cale Yarborough, who had been alternating the lead, knew that whoever made it back to the finish line first would be the winner. So they hurtled toward the line at nearly 200 miles (322 km) per hour. They bumped once, then again, and then again! In the end, Petty got to the line ahead of Yarborough by about the width of a fender.

Yarborough (left) and Petty bump doors as they sprint to the finish of the Firecracker 400.

Green-White-Checkered

For the safety of its drivers, NASCAR has eliminated "racing to the caution." In the case of the 1984 Firecracker 400, many drivers had already slowed down when Petty and Yarborough were making their wild chase. Now, when a caution flag comes out, the field is "frozen" in the order that the cars already are in. But a finish under a caution flag under those circumstances would be downright boring to fans at the track and watching on television. So if a caution flag comes out near the end of a race, NASCAR now has a restart consisting of two laps called a "Green-White-Checkered Finish." The green flag means that the restart is on, and there are two laps left. The white flag means that it's the final lap. And the checkered flag signals the winner. It makes for an exciting sprint to the finish!

Hail to the Chief

The 1984 Firecracker 400 was significant not only because it was the 200th career victory for legendary driver Richard Petty, but also because it marked the first time that a sitting U.S. President attended a NASCAR race. Ronald Reagan gave the starting call via phone from Air Force One— "Gentlemen, start your engines!"— then watched much of the action from the press box.

President Ronald Reagan was among the fans thrilled by the 1984 Firecracker 400.

17

The Stuff of Legends

There's an old saying in sports that great players make great plays in great games. Well, great drivers do their thing in great races. These legends of the sport built, or cemented, their reputations in these races.

The 'Intimidator' Roars Back

Dale Earnhardt Sr. already was a legend by the time he lined up for the Winston 500 at the Talladega Superspeedway in Talladega, Alabama, in October of 2000. His record-tying seven NASCAR championships and his hard-charging, back-down-to-no-one driving style had earned him crowds of fans. But late in this race, few people in the crowd of more than 130,000 expected that Earnhardt would add to his previous 75 career victories. After all, he stood in 18th place just five laps from the finish. A victory seemed out of the question. But it had been a wild and crazy day at a wild and crazy racetrack.

The lead changed hands 46 times in the race, alternating among 21 different drivers. So Earnhardt never took his eyes off the prize. He couldn't get around the cars, which were running three-wide, on the outside. So he tried the middle. He passed one car, then another, then another. With two laps to go, Earnhardt was behind only three other drivers, one of whom was his son, Dale Jr. Dale Sr. passed all three before the last lap began, then held on to win.

It's the Man in Black! Dale Earnhardt Sr. was one of NASCAR's legendary drivers.

18

"The Pass in the Grass"

In 1984, Dale Earnhardt Sr. made another big comeback—from 23rd place with 13 laps to go—to win the Talladega 500. But it was his "Pass in the Grass" at the 1987 Winston (NASCAR's all-star race) that really made him a legend. Late in the race, Earnhardt and Bill Elliott bumped each other several times while Earnhardt was trying to hold on to the lead. The last bump sent Earnhardt to the infield grass. He steadied the car, kept the lead—technically, there was no pass involved—and ran Elliott up toward the wall. He wasn't going to take any rough tactics without answering. And, oh by the way, Earnhardt went on to win the race, too!

No. 3's Last Win

No one knew it at the time, of course, but Dale Earnhardt Sr.'s victory in the 2000 Winston 500 turned out to be the final one of his remarkable career. There were only four races left in the 2000 season. He didn't win any of them, although he did finish second in the season-ending Napa 500, and was second in the overall standings. In the following year's season-opening Daytona 500, Earnhardt was killed in a crash on the last turn of the last lap.

Few sights were as intimidating to a driver as seeing Dale Earnhardt Sr.'s black No. 3 car in the rearview mirror. Of course, lots of times he was out in front, too!

19

Slingshot

They called David Pearson "The Fox" for his cunning on the track. Pearson used that intelligence—and his natural driving ability—to win 105 races in a long career that spanned from 1960 to 1986. Only Richard Petty, with 200 career victories, took the checkered flag in a NASCAR race more often than Pearson did. The best example of Pearson's racing smarts came in the 1974 Firecracker 400. Knowing that his only chance to win would be to come from behind on the last lap, he purposely let Richard Petty take the lead, then utilized a "slingshot" pass to win at the end. Petty and Pearson were long-time rivals, and Petty usually had the upper hand—just as he did, more often than not, over every other driver on the track. On this day at the Daytona International Speedway, the two superstar drivers were battling neck and neck for the lead late in the race. On the final lap, Pearson was in the lead. The trouble was, he felt that whoever was in second place near the end would take advantage of the **aerodynamics** and slingshot past the other driver to win. So Pearson slowed down and drifted to the left. Thinking that his rival must be out of gas, Petty zoomed by. But Pearson was back up to speed in an instant. He got up on Petty's bumper and stayed there until the final turn, then made his "slingshot" pass to win by a car length.

Petty (43) and Pearson (21) were frequent rivals. This photo is from a race in 1977.

Good Thinking

At first, Petty was mad at Pearson over what happened. Petty even went up into the press box after the race to seek out Pearson, who was talking to reporters about his big win. "David usually drives a safer and saner race," Petty told the media. He felt like Pearson had made a dangerous move that could have wrecked them both—while each of them was racing along at more than 180 miles (289.7 km) per hour. More likely, though, Petty was just angry and embarrassed that he had been tricked. In fact, over time, he came to admire the ploy. The only problem? "I wish I had thought of it," Petty said.

That's Davey Allison (left) sharing a laugh with his father Bobby Allison before a race.

All in the Family

The Pearsons and the Pettys are two of the more prominent racing families in NASCAR history. Another is the Allison family. When Bobby Allison won the 1988 Daytona 500 by just two car lengths, he held off his son, Davey, who finished second.

Nice Guys Finish First

When Bill Elliott had a chance to win a $1 million bonus going into the Southern 500 at Darlington in 1985, just about the whole NASCAR community was rooting for him.

A Crown Jewel

In 1950, the Southern 500 first was held at Darlington Raceway in Darlington, South Carolina. The race soon became one of the four "Crown Jewels" of NASCAR. The others were the Daytona 500, the Winston 500, and the World 600. For more than half a century, through the 2004 season, the Southern 500 was one of the highlights on the NASCAR schedule. (A legal dispute dropped it off the schedule after that).

In 1985, NASCAR **sponsor** Winston offered a bonus of $1 million to any driver who could win three of the four Crown Jewels in the same season. It was great publicity for Winston. It was great incentive for NASCAR drivers, too. Still, winning three of the biggest races on the schedule seemed almost impossible. And history indicated that Winston probably wouldn't have to worry about writing out the extra check.

That's Bill Elliott in the No. 9 Dodge. He had a million reasons to celebrate his victory in the Southern 500 at Darlington Raceway in 1985.

Mr. Popularity

Bill Elliott is one of the top drivers in NASCAR history. He's also one of the most popular. This chart shows the men who have won the fan-friendly sport's prestigious Most Popular Driver Award more than one time:

Driver	Most Popular Awards
Bill Elliott	16
Bobby Allison	8
Richard Petty	8
Dale Earnhardt Jr.	4
Fred Lorenzen	2
Darrell Waltrip	2

Million-Dollar Bill

The very first year of the bonus, however, Bill Elliott had a chance at the prize. He opened the 1985 season by winning the Daytona 500 in February. Three months later, he took the checkered flag at the Winston 500 at Talladega. He was already two-thirds of the way to a million dollars and there were two "Crown Jewel" races still to go! Elliott finished well back at the World 600 on May 26, settling for 18th place. So his final chance at becoming an instant millionaire was at the Southern 500 on September 1. Elliott was in a good position from the start of the race, having qualified with the fastest time. But it took 367 laps to go 500 miles (804.7 km) around the 1.4 mile (2.2 km) oval at Darlington, and many of those

Bill Elliott is as good a driver as he is a good guy. In a career that began in 1976—he still drove a limited schedule in 2007—he's won 44 races and nearly $40 million in prize money.

turns were harrowing. In a crash-filled race, Elliott narrowly missed wrecking his car on several occasions. At the end, only three cars were on their final lap. Cale Yarborough, who had won the Southern 500 five times, chased Elliott to the end, but came up six-tenths of a second short. Elliott won the bonus. The million dollars nicely added to the $53,725 Elliott took home as first prize for the race. And Elliott became a legend known as "Million-Dollar Bill."

Pedal to the Metal

Every racecar driver has the same goal: to take the checkered flag. So when the flag is in sight, it's time to give it everything he's got. And sometimes, it's not only a race on the line, but also a championship in the balance.

One, two, three! These stock cars are zooming along door-to-door at high speed.

Three Cars, Two Feet!

Fierce flag-to-flag racing has been Talladega's trademark since the superspeedway opened in 1969. In fact, some of NASCAR's wildest races ever have taken place there. There was the time in 1984, for instance, when the lead went back and forth among 13 different drivers a record 75 times. And the race in 2000, when Dale Earnhardt Sr. found himself in 18th place with only five laps to go. Earnhardt never gave up, though, and he roared back to win. That kind of nonstop action has made Talladega one of the favorite tracks among NASCAR fans. No one knows what will happen until the checkered flag waves. Take the 1981 UAW-Ford 500, for example. In an unmatched one-two-three finish, rookie Ron Bouchard overtook Darrell Waltrip and Terry Labonte in the final 500 yards (457 m) of the 500 mile (805 km) race. Bouchard won by less than a foot over Waltrip. Labonte was less than another foot behind.

Baker Stuns Earnhardt

There have been lots of other dramatic finishes in NASCAR history—too many to mention them all here. One of the best came at the Winston 500 at Talladega in 1980. Dale Earnhardt Sr. was still a young driver making his way in stock car racing when veteran Buddy Baker made a thrilling stretch run to pull off a stunning victory. Earnhardt led late in the race, but Baker overcame a 16-second **deficit** over the final three laps. "I drafted every car in sight," he said afterwards. Baker sped an incredible 202 miles (325 km) per hour on the final stretch, and he won by three feet (0.9 meters).

Let's Go to the Video Tape

In 1990, Davey Allison held off hard-charging Mark Martin by six inches (15 cm) at the finish of the Valleydale 500. It was so close that NASCAR officials had to go back and watch video tape before they could announce who won the race. One year later, Allison was on the other end of a close battle, falling to Dale Jarrett by just 10 inches (25 cm) in the 1991 Champion Spark Plug 400. But that wasn't even a close call compared to Ricky Craven's victory over Kurt Busch at Darlington in the 2003 season. In the closest race ever, Craven won by .002 seconds—that's just two-thousandths of one second!

Watch closely! It's incredible that after 400 or 500 miles (644 or 805 km) of driving, the difference between first and second place might be only inches.

Down to the Wire

Points leader Davey Allison needed to finish fifth or better in the season's final race in Hampton, Georgia, to win the 1992 NASCAR title. But 74 laps from the end of the 328-lap Hooters 500, his hopes were dashed by a crash. He finished the race in 27th place, and dropped to third for the season. That left Bill Elliott and Alan Kulwicki to battle for the championship, and they soon were racing in first and second place. Kulwicki needed to win the race to capture the season title. Elliott needed to win the race and lead the most laps. (NASCAR awards a five-point bonus to the driver who leads the most laps in a given race). With 18 laps to go, Kulwicki was in front, but he had to go in for a pit stop. While Kulwicki was getting gas and new tires, Elliott took over the lead, and held on to win the race. But who won the season championship?

Alan Kulwicki knew just what he needed to do to win the 1992 season points championship.

A Big Bonus

Elliott won the battle (the race), but Kulwicki won the war (the season title). Kulwicki led 103 laps of the Hooters 500, while Elliott led 102. The five bonus points gave Kulwicki 4,078 points in the season standings; Elliott finished with 4,068 points. If Elliott had gotten the five bonus points instead, they both would have finished with 4,073 points, and Elliott would have been declared the champion because he had won more races over the course of the season.

End of One Era...

The final race of the 1992 season was one of the most exciting days in NASCAR history. Not only did the points championship come down to the wire (as noted on the previous page), but all-time wins leader Richard Petty was racing for the last time in his storied career. Things didn't go quite as Petty might have planned it: He was involved in a six-car pileup early on in the race, and his car caught fire. "Guess I went out in a blaze of glory," the seven-time NASCAR champion joked. "That really wasn't the way I meant to go."

Richard Petty shows the fans he's okay after his crash. While Petty's career was winding down, Jeff Gordon's (right) was just getting started.

...Start of a New One

At the same time that Richard Petty was winding down his legendary career at the 1992 Hooters 500, an upstart rookie named Jeff Gordon was just beginning his career. The 21-year-old Gordon made his Cup Series debut in the race at Atlanta. Gordon wasn't a factor in the race—he finished 31st. But stock car fans everywhere soon would know his name.

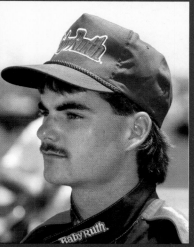

The Chase Is On

This was just what NASCAR officials hoped for when they changed the scoring system to include a playoff chase for the first time in the 2004 season: a memorable finish to a memorable season.

A New Era

Up until 2004, NASCAR's champion simply was the driver who accumulated the most points over the course of the entire season. That meant that every race was just as important as any other in the final standings—but it also meant that sometimes the champion was pretty much decided long before the end of the season, which wasn't very exciting. But in the first year of the new points system (see page 29), several drivers entered the last race of 2004 in Homestead, Florida, with a chance at the season championship. And as the Ford 400 progressed, the projected final standings were in constant flux. The race kept stock car fans on the edge of their seats to the very end.

So Close

The closest that any two drivers were going into the last race of the season was in 1979. Richard Petty trailed Darrell Waltrip by two points that year. But then Petty finished fifth in the Los Angeles Times 500 while Waltrip was eighth. That was enough to give "The King" his seventh title by an 11-point margin.

And the Winner Is...

Kurt Busch entered the Ford 400 with an 18-point lead in the overall standings, but a whole bunch of drivers—Jimmie Johnson, Jeff Gordon, Dale Earnhardt Jr., and Mark Martin—were all positioned to catch him. Just a few spots up or down in the final race would make the difference. So it looked like a disaster for Busch when he

In the 2004 Ford 400, Kurt Busch kept his eye on the prize: the season title.

lost a tire about a third of the way into the Ford 400. He kept his car from crashing, but he fell to 28th place in the race—and out of first place overall—by the time he got the wheel fixed. But Busch, who was only 26 years old at the time and in his fourth full season in NASCAR's Cup Series, knew that he still had a chance, so he never gave up. Busch steadily climbed back into the top 10. In the end, he was in fifth place in the day's race. Greg Biffle held off Jimmie Johnson to take the checkered flag. But Busch's finish was enough to give him a narrow, eight-point victory over Johnson in the season standings. It was the closest finish ever.

The Points System

NASCAR determines its season champion with a system that awards points for every race during the season. The winner of each race gets 185 points. Second place gets 170 points, and third place gets 165 points. The total keeps going down in increments of five, four, or three points on down to 34 points for 43rd, or last place. In addition, five bonus points are awarded to any driver who leads a lap during the race, and five more to the driver who leads the most laps. After 26 races of the 36-race schedule, the top 12 drivers in the standings have their points reset to 5,000 (plus bonus points for races won). Those drivers then compete in the 10-race "Chase for the Sprint Cup." Those races are still full, 43-driver fields, and points are awarded to everyone on the track, but only those 12 can earn enough points to win the championship. The driver with the most points at the end of the "Chase" earns his place in history!

Road Trip!

Road courses are different from the ovals on which NASCAR drivers usually race. These courses present a special test that can make for a memorable race.

Just Like the Old Days!

For NASCAR fans who enjoy road-course races, the Centurion Boats at the Glen in 2007 was one to remember. But you didn't have to be a road-course fan to appreciate Tony Stewart's victory. Race fans of all kinds were thrilled at the no-holds-barred, give-it-all-you've-got action in Watkins Glen, New York. It was **reminiscent** of stock-car racing's early days on tracks in the dirt and the sand. The race even featured a pushing and yelling match on the track between Kevin Harvick and Juan Pablo Montoya, who were involved in a crash late in the race. Harvick got out of his car and walked over to Montoya. Harvick blamed Montoya for the crash that got his car. Montoya said that it wasn't his fault. The two men nearly came to blows in front of the fans—and folks watching on TV!

A Big Mistake

With only a few races to go before the "Chase for the Cup," several drivers were trying to position themselves for NASCAR's playoffs when they raced at Watkins Glen in 2007. Jeff Gordon, however, was not one of those drivers. With a playoff spot pretty much all wrapped up, all Gordon had on his mind was adding to his NASCAR-record nine career wins on road courses. And for most of the day, Gordon was out front. But with Stewart close behind and less than two laps to go, Gordon made a mistake. He took a turn too fast and spun out, falling to ninth place.

There's a lot more than just four left turns on a road course. The challenging track means some exciting racing that fans love to watch.

Types of Tracks

NASCAR races are held on four different types of track: **superspeedways**, **intermediate tracks**, **short courses**, and **road courses**. The superspeedways (such as the famous Daytona International Speedway) are the largest ovals. They're more than two miles (3.2 km) in length and feature steep banks and high speeds. Intermediate tracks are between one (1.6 km) and two miles (3.2 km) in length. Short courses are ovals that are less than one mile (1.6 km) long. Road courses aren't ovals at all, but feature right turns as well as left turns. The only stops on the NASCAR schedule on road courses are in Sonoma, California, and Watkins Glen, New York.

Victory or Bust

Because of Jeff Gordon's rare error, it appeared that Tony Stewart would win easily—until Carl Edwards came roaring up from behind and got right on Stewart's bumper. Edwards had his eye only on the checkered flag. "I didn't want to finish second," Edwards said. On the last lap, he tried to floor it past Stewart, but went off flying into the gravel pit between the drivers and the spectators. He recovered to finish eighth. Stewart won, and Denny Hamlin finished in second place.

Wipeout! Jeff Gordon (24) spins out of control late in the race at Watkins Glen in 2007. Tony Stewart (20) sped by and went on to win.

Glossary

aerodynamics The motion of air and how it affects other bodies (in this case, how knowledge of it can be used to make a race car go faster!)

caution flag One of several colored flags that NASCAR officials use to signal drivers during a race. The caution flag is yellow and means that there has been a wreck or other hazardous situation; cars must slow down and remain in their order in single file behind the leader

chassis The steel "skeleton" of a car

cockpit The place where the driver sits

controversy Differences of opinion over what really happened

deficit Shortage; in this case, it means being behind in a race

governing body A person or group that is in charge; in sports, a governing body makes the rules, sets the schedule, and settles disputes

gutsy Something that takes courage, or nerve

intimidator Someone who fills someone else with fear by his or her presence or actions

open-wheel A type of racecar that has a tube-shaped body and wheels that are not covered by fenders on the cars body

reminiscent An event that brings to mind an earlier event

rookie A first-year competitor in a professional sport

sentimental Having to do with feelings or emotions

sponsor A company that gives money to a person or team in exchange for promotions of the company's products or services

stock car An automobile made in a factory and available for purchase by the general public

veteran A person who has a lot of experience or practice in an activity

Index